DIVINE STYLE
VS.
DEMONIC WORDPLAY

DIVINE STYLE
VS.
DEMONIC WORDPLAY

NK BWANA

Order this book online at www.trafford.com
or email orders@trafford.com

Most Trafford titles are also available at major online book retailers.

Printed in the United States of America.

ISBN: 978-1-4120-5792-9 (sc)

Library of Congress Control Number: 2011913320

Trafford rev. 05/24/2013

North America & international
toll-free: 1 888 232 4444 (USA & Canada)
phone: 250 383 6864 ◆ fax: 812 355 4082

CONTENTS

Truest Measure of a Man 3

Been So Long 9

Numbered Days 14

Survive Until Prevail 17

Since 1 Negro Hero Must Go To War 24

All Blacked Out and Still, Not Televised 28

Fighting to Become Reborn 34

Funk-Nastyfied Changes for Jonny T 40

Seated at the Right Hand 43

Less Than I ever Wanted 47

Funk-Nastyfied Nervous Laughter for Erin Powers 50

No Se Ch**ga con a Still-Born Infant's Piercing Demands por
    Representacion 54

See, You Still Ain't Moved 60

I Hunger 4 Thee 66

Come, as I Do (You) 70

Funk-Nastyfied England, Keep My Bones 77

One in A Million Tarnished Eyes & Sapphire Knuckles 80

Yes I am, Yes I Can 88

Thoughts Flow Like Piss 94

Misfits of the Cracked, Chapped, Dry Lips 97

While Thoughts Linger 101

My get Out of Hell Free Card 107

Harbored Vessels of Contempt 112

Midwifing Movements 117

Night That Simultaneously Beat Hearts (rewind time) 123

Azure Moods & Mocha Kisses 128

Write For I 135

BY WAY OF ACKNOWLEDGMENT:

I wish I could simply acknowledge and dedicate this book A las Mujeres or To the Women like Sandra Cisneros, but I would be remiss if I did.

First and foremost, this book goes to Mom, Auntie, Pati, Mama and "All of Them" for their unwavering inspiration, sufficient guidance and unconditional support.

To Kikesa, Cuatli and Kiese for their creative being and undeniable becoming reflection of the best of my intentions and aspirations.

To Tawe, Gloria and Robert, Mercy-Faith and Brian, Bentley and Leila, Gabriel, Manny, Aisha, Sam, Dave, Grandma Henri and Grandpa Mike, Pops and the rest of my dear friends and family who are always with me.

To the Original Black Arts Movement pioneers (especially Zora Neale Hurston, Langston Hughes, Paul Laurence Dunbar, Countee Cullen and Claude McKay) and revolutionary minds who took unique circumstances and inevitable sarcasm and created magnificent, rich, complicated and entertaining work while teaching us to make a rhythm stressing "talking don't amount to much, if it's divorced from experience".

To Alice Walker, Gwendolyn Brooks, June Jordan, Rita Dove, Nikki Giovanni and the current truth-tellers, preachers, teachers, poets and healers burdened with the obligation of revealing the interconnected network of linguistic, intellectual, ethical, moral, social, emotional, psychological and physical attitudes and actions that we have had to endure while still loving ourselves when we are laughing . . . . and then again when we are looking mean and impressive.

Ultimately, this book is dedicated to like-minded activists, readers, universal global citizens and spirits. To those who intricately and intimately understand we may celebrate nearly 50 years after the Voting Rights Act and squarely 50 years after the Civil Rights Act, even with a Black Family in the White House, we are still separate and unequal even at home sweet home sophisticatedly altered from life, liberty and the pursuit of happiness.

Since life still truly ain't been no crystal stair, I pray that my attempt is validated and cherished instead of confusing obscurity with depth.

1. A ghost of a fraction of the captivating "macaroni" charm of Eldridge Cleaver melts my *Soul on Ice* and radiates through me

Precious Reader,

Our majority racist, sexist opportunistic, capitalistic society forces us to become proficient at "making lemonade". In the process, Divine Style vs Demonic Word Play.docx you must find your self, your values, your beliefs. What is greatness? What is worthy of praise and remembrance? What characteristics do we want to embody and pass on to future generations through our true lasting heroes'?

TRUEST MEASURE OF A MAN

A ghost of a fraction of the
Energetic rebellious essence of **Nat Turner**
Endures in Me

A ghost of a fraction of the
Agitating dignified eloquence of **Frederick Douglass**
Influences Me

A ghost of a fraction of the
Authentic brilliance of **George Washington Carver**
Corresponds with Me

A ghost of a fraction of the
Freethinking revolutionary vision of **Marcus Garvey**
Instigates Me

A ghost of a fraction of the
Undisputed champion & legendary nobility of **Jesse Owens**
Prevails in Me

A ghost of a fraction of the
Insightful integrity of **Thoroughgood Marshall**
Adjudicates Me

A ghost of a fraction of the
Symbolic leadership & selfless martyrdom of **Patrice Lumumba**
Abides in Me

A ghost of a fraction of the
Permanent passion & pride of **Halle Selassie**
Surges through Me

A ghost of a fraction of the
Independent expressive complexity of **Malcolm X**
Occupies Me

A ghost of a fraction of the
Astounding versatile ability of **Muhammad Ali**
Stimulates Me

A ghost of a fraction of the
Misunderstood, black-hearts, white lies,
Wordsmith in **Langston Hughes**
Drifts through Me

A ghost of a fraction of the
Inclusive definitions & expanded expressiveness of **Alvin Ailey**
Breaths in Me

A ghost of a fraction of the
Pioneering courage, risk & loneliness of **Jackie Robinson**
Exists in Me

A ghost of a fraction of the
Artistic creative defiance of **Miles Davis**
Seduces Me

A ghost of a fraction of the
Captivating "macaroni" charm of **Eldridge Cleaver**
Melts my "Soul on Ice" and radiates through Me

A ghost of a fraction of the
Evident activism of **Jim Brown**
Defines Me

A ghost of a fraction of the
Provocative political consciousness of **Bob Marley**
Articulates through Me

A ghost of a fraction of the
Reflective soulful communicative imagination of **Marvin Gaye**
Survives in Me

A ghost of a fraction of the
Justified patience of **Nelson Mandela**
Swells through Me

A ghost of a fraction of the
Genuine humility & miscalculated grace of **Arthur Ashe**
Continues exponentially through Me

A ghost of a fraction of the
Raw pure explosiveness of **Mike Tyson**
Satiates Me

A ghost of a fraction of the
Apparent carefree thug-passion tendency of **Tupac Shakur**
Resounds in Me

A ghost of a fraction of the
Heroic tangible father-figure &
Brightest guiding example of the
Truest measure of the purest manner
Of the actual man found in my Mother
Dorote Mingienze Bwana Matondo Ilaka
Multiplies through Me

Honestly & actually
A ghost of a fraction of You and Me
Is defined, combined & refined by You and Me

If these independent, disenfranchised and fractional entities
Are NOT interdependent, franchised actual
representatives of Me
Or my boundless capacity

Then how else should I prove I am?
I am.
I AM!

2. *Trying to bring concrete depictions, convictions, definitions, of nonfiction diction along*

Precious Reader,

This is my humble attempt at an overdue apology for not doing anything proactive or preventative. An admission of guilt for being a silent partner to the demise of Hip Hop, Poetry, Art & Culture and artistic endeavors of vision and innovation. My prayer is that my apology will be accepted and my invitation valued as a step in a gap-filling direction.

BEEN SO LONG

May the blessings from the
Forbidden Precision Funk Nasty Spell flow

Far beyond
The soulful apology for so long
Being gone
And not leaving you anything
In the meantime to hold on
To the hope and memory
Of artistic creativity & linguistic ability forgone

Dry your eyes
Baby
Live in the flesh is
Double Duty a.k.a. Funk Nasty

Your abstract lyrics and
Concrete delivery daddy's home
P.S.
Yes
I sincerely apologize and
need you to know
I know
You know
I know
It's Been
So
Long

It's been so long since you heard a skilled M.C.
Holding sh** down
most definitely

It's been so long since you heard a skilled M.C.
Holding sh** down
most definitely
Been so long

It's been so long
Since a hero unsung
Spoken Word poet
Came strong
And begun to unspun
What was left
Undone
Why, when, and where
Hip-Hop went
Wrong

Most wordsmiths got
Hung
Trying to bring
Concrete depictions, convictions
Definitions
Of nonfiction diction
Along
It's been so
Long
But don't get me
Wrong

Don't try to repress, depress, or
Suppress the subject
The *Forbidden Precision* C.D.

Is on point and on
Hit
It's the perfect Hip-Hop, Jazz, Spoken Word
Balanced fit
In fact it's the
Illerrific verbal composition
Plus
Pineal linguistic gymnastics and
Antics
That elevates the
Forbidden Precision
Tactics
Of the Poetical Prophet Jonny T. and
Double Duty the Afrikanized
Funk Nasty creative practice

Guaranteed to catch
Wreck
Funk Nasty's on
Deck
Forbidden Precision is what's
Next and
Poetic lyrical fusion history is
The rest

3. *I'm only here till the devil wakes up*
   From his slumber

Precious Reader,

This piece originally began as a quick write exercise. This found poem was rescued from the garbage can because it spoke to me with piercing clarity. Life isn't about what happens to you, but how you respond when you are tested with trials and tribulations. How will you respond?

Numbered Days

My days on this wretched earth are numbered

I'm only here till the devil wakes up from her slumber

She tells me to get my black ass back to work

Down under

and

"Leave the godda** refreshing glass of ice water,

Mother

Fu**er"

4. When the universally culturally,
   politically-correct and accepted norm
   Doesn't comply with your definitions,
   experiences tone, depth, hue, shape or form

Precious Reader,

Your faith is supposed to be tested or else how else would you know that it was faith. Often, it takes all of our energy to just keep on "keeping on," or be sick and tired of "being sick and tired." The difference between champions and general participants, is that we persevere until the tables turn, until the odds crumble, and we are destined to triumph over former crushing obstacles.

SURVIVE UNTIL PREVAIL

Survive until Prevail
When sacrilegious sentiments
strangle, suffocate and satiate
sound systems and sane situations

Survive until Prevail
When grotesque glamorization's,
contrived reenactments,
and miniscule misunderstandings
perpetuate and escalate
from homicidal idolizations
to secure attempts of suicidal ideation

Survive until Prevail
When innocent illusory sexual flirtations
associate with unanswered persuasions
that propel potential positive possession
of pepper spray

While guilty lingering sexual harassment convictions
invite unwelcome advances
and penetrations

Survive until Prevail
When you are psychologically and
spiritually forced to marry
guilt, shame, pain, neglect and abuse

Cause Shatan (Satan) got multitudes of
stock and investments in you,
While it seems Allah (Creator) done forgot you

Survive until Prevail
When the living dead
attempt to simplify & categorize deep meditations
And white out, zero out & nullify
original creations

Survive until Prevail,
When the universally and culturally,
Politically correct, and accepted norm
Doesn't comply with your definitions, experiences,
tone, depth, hue, shape or form

Survive until Prevail
When your ideal, soul-mate and genuine true love
Regenerated into a
hysterical, pathetic, shallow,
tarnished and fragmented mirage

Survive until Prevail
When your multiple, pure, holy and virgin seeds
Are diabolically stretched and trapped between
custody, legal status, visitation, divorce, greed,
lies, deceit and all things impure and unclean

Survival until Prevail
When a transparent angel
makes herself available to you
and states that she'll **"pray for you"**

The curve of her gaze state
that she'll patiently wait
stimulate and recidivate
life, joy, and hope in you

But the card states
that she'll **"pray for you"**
she'll **"pray for you"**

The curve of her smile explains
that she'll curiously wait
stimulate and reintegrate
ironic invitations, compassionate presentations
cerebral convulsions,
and sensational celebrations

But the card states
that she'll **"pray for you"**
she'll **"pray for you"**
"pray for you"

The curve of her spine proclaims
that she will willingly unwind
captivatingly recline
titillatingly moan, calculatingly bump,
and mercilessly grind
Until we capture & control infinite complexity of
Creative imagination, confined space and concurrent time
But the card states
that she'll **"pray for you"**
she'll **"pray for you"**
"pray for you"
"for you"
"you"

Therefore, either I am in desperate need of an intense
remedial refresher course in
Gaze Comprehension, Smile Interpretation
and Spine Application and

She truly merely wishes to
"pray for me"
Or

She hopelessly needs
to allow her will and essence to reveal
What her heart, mind and soul
Betrayingly conceal

Ironically, the powers that be
have foreseen
With keen precision and supreme vision
that she needs
More prayers for herself
to release
communally
Than she could ever reasonably deliver on my behalf
virtually and exponentially
Believe you me

Survive until Prevail
When the lone condition of children
Mandate you

Survive until Prevail
When the rustic reincarnate choice of decency or chivalry
Obligate you

Survive until Prevail
When the purposeful positive pursuit of justice
Suffocate you

Survive until Prevail
When the jubilant joy of pleasure
Adjudicate you

Survive until Prevail
When the sacred security of peace
Encapsulate you

Survive until Prevail
When the potential of experiencing the sacred
Perpetuate you

Survive until Prevail
When the evidence of things hoped for yet unseen
Consecrate you

Survive until Prevail
When the critical conversion of suffocating nightmares
Convert into reassuring cool breezes of unpolluted air

Oxygenating
your gland-pineal

Electrifyingly resurrecting
the sanctity of your structure

Solidifying
the soundness of your spiritual

Projecting
the purposeful validity of your physical

Masquerading
the multi-dimensional, multiple masterpieces and mission
of your mental

Survive until Prevail
Survive
Prevail

5. **I go to war with my
    blue-balled style pen and
    with my sterile futile pad**

Precious Reader,

Every artistic endeavor takes commitment, sacrifice and struggle far beyond what the common person could acknowledge or critique. Every champion must first conquer her own internal demons and apprehensions before we can capture our goals, dreams or aspirations. Since the worthy struggle continues, our capacity and sustaining will must continue forever plus one day. Beware, it's usually not the forever that takes you out, rather, it is in the constant pending details of that additional 24 hour day. That final day robs us and is capable of castrating and decapitating the best of intentions, the noblest of causes, and the final drop of exhausted resources. Stay laced-up, strapped-up and ready at attention to go to war and come back whole.

Since 1 Negro Hero Must Go To War

Since one Negro hero
Must go
To war
I go
To
War

I go to war daily
Continually and habitually
I go to war with my
Agile mind
With my
Fragile emotions
With my
Blue-balled style pen and
With my
Sterile futile pad

I go to war
To protect and serve
The possibility and opportunity
That each
Humble sensation creative expression
Might breath
Distinctively, independently and indefinitely
Enjoying the freedom and responsibility
Of the LIFE
I've truly
Never had

Since one Negro hero
Must go
To war

War I go to
To War I go
Go to War I
I go to War

6. The revolution will not be right back after a brainwashing of white innocence, white privilege, white guilt, white lies or white weddings

Precious Reader,

Ralph Waldo Emerson stated, "Every revolution was once a single thought in one man's mind." I suppose you could say that at this point in my life both my thoughts and terrors are of our societies addiction to solely promoting sex, drugs and violence. It appears there is no vision and direction of healing, renewal, preservation of humanity, kindness, consideration or mercy. The more things change, the more they have remained the same.

ALL BLACKED OUT AND STILL, NOT TELEVISED

You won't be able to
Remain unconscious any longer Brothers and Sisters

You won't be able to
Post, upgrade, download, email, tweet, text message or instant message

You won't be able to
Unwind and recline on Mary Jane lucid
While flying and frying your mind
On crystal meth or acid
Because the Revolution still
Will not be televised

The Revolution may be all blacked out and still, not televised

It will not be brought to you live
By Nike, Nokia, or Tostito's

There will be no commercial sponsors
For Lewinsky deep throat lozenges
Arnolds Hummers
Or the "Commander" in some nut-huggers
Holding a fighter flight helmet on the S.S. Abraham Lincoln
Because the Revolution still
Will not be televised

The Revolution may be all blacked out and still, not televised

It will not be brought to you
By the Apollo, Pantages, Broadway or Kodak Theater

Starring Tom Sawyer, Tom Cruise, Tom Hanks,
Jim Carey, Denzel or Halle Berry

The Revolution will not give stretch marks sex appeal
Or get rid of the pool of sweat from the fat on your back

The revolution will not make you appear lighter on D.V.D
Or make you definitely sound whiter on C.D
Because the Revolution still
Will not be televised
The Revolution may be all blacked out and still, not televised

There will be no pictures of
Another Mike Tyson first-round knock out
Kobe buzzer beater
Or Tiger Woods birdie on the 18th tee

No video trailers of
Trailer trash on COPs
Police chases on the I-10
Or Drive by shooting mother's victims desperate please

Please no pictures of
Madonna tonguing Brittany
Timberlake handprints on Janet's titty (breast)
Paris Hilton vaginally, orally or anally
Wedding vow renewals at rehab for Bobby and Whitney
Or G.W. swallowing Powell while spooning Cheney
Because the Revolution still
Will not be televised

The Revolution may be all blacked out and still, not televised

Elimidate, 5th Wheel, Survivor, Tosh point O, TMZ, Jersey Shore and the Bachelor
Won't be so damn relevant or reality TV

Gossip whores won't even care if
Benjamin is getting puffy
While Gigolo is giving Puffy "puffy"
Because the Revolution still
Will not be televised

There will be no
Late breaking news this just in
No this is just a test
Of the emergency broadcast system
No chronological biographies
Of Saddam Hussein, Osama Bin Laden
Jean Bertrand Aristide or Fidel Castro

The theme song will not
Be written by Willie Nelson, Kenny Rogers or Dolly Parton
Nor will it be performed live via satellite
By Beyoncé, the Dixie Chicks, Rhianna, Jessica Simpson or Kelley Clarkson
Because the Revolution still
Will not be televised

The Revolution
Will not be televised
Will not be televised
will Not be televised
Will not be televised
will not Be televised
Will not be televised
will not be Televised

The Revolution will not
Strike back through e-mails, recall petitions, sit-ins, teach-ins or boycotts

The Revolution will have no pause, delete, edit or re-play functions
The Revolution will have no pause, delete, edit or re-play functions

Brothers and Sisters the Revolution will be
All the way live and direct
With God-speed, maximum force and full
Effect

7. There's only one gold medalist, no silver, no bronze and 999,999 coulda, woulda, shoulda competitors, buried together with the womb tomb as their final resting place

Precious Reader,

This is actually my first published piece on the road to recovery and the discovery of my intimate love affair with dull pencils and bland pages of legal paper, napkins, tissue paper, toilet paper, the palm of my hand, etcetera. I dedicate it to all the "lounge cats and foxy kittens" who always knew what they wanted to be when they "grew up," but somehow someway became disconnected from that initial dream and vision as life transpired. This is for the countless relegated individuals who feel destitute, unfulfilled and alone in a regulated routine between then and here and now desperately plead for another chance at hope, another chance at joy, another chance at peace and another opportunity for unconditional love.

FIGHTING TO BECOME REBORN

Sometimes like death
Is the sole possibility
Of loaning life indefinitely
To a **dead soul**

Somehow like death
Is the sole possibility
Of sparking thoughts instinctively
To a **comatose mind**

Someway like death
Is the sole possibility
Of translating voice audibly to a **mute tongue**

But this here
Spoken Word Salvation exists
As the proverbial egg
Deep inside the birth canal

The sole surviving egg that
Millions of sperm embark on that long lonely
Journey of longing, hoping, praying, and enduring
Enduring to reach the finish line in time
In time to collect the fruits of their labor
Be revived and catapulted to survival

For this Russian roulette
This Russian roulette is truly do or die
There is only 1 gold medalist,
No silver, no bronze and 999,999
Coulda, woulda, shoulda competitors
Buried together

With the womb-tomb
As their final
Resting place

Even second place
Don't get a V.IP. burial
At the top of the mound
Because the life-supporting egg can only caress and develop
One Champion

This Champion contains
All of the life force capable of
Resurrecting non-believers by performing the miracle of
Representing the mute with only
One Word

This Champion contains
All of the life force capable of
Resurrecting non-believers by performing the miracle of
Redirecting the mind with only
One Line

This Champion contains
All of the life force capable of
Resurrecting non-believers by performing the miracle of
Recessitating the heart with only
One Phrase

This Champion contains
All of the life force capable of
Resurrecting non-believers by performing the miracle of
Rekindling the soul with only
One Thought

The eternal life of every poem is
Sanctioned and sanctified every time

In the name of,
Like minds in unlike phases of comprehension
Unite

In the name of,
Like languages in unlike dialects of communication
Unite

In the name of,
Like hearts in unlike contexts of coercions
Unite

In the name of,
Like souls in unlike planes of catharsis
Unite

Unite, unite, unite and
Reunite
To this union and communion
Enabling us to
Escape the snare of death

Enabling us to
Escape the glare of lies

Allowing us to
Accept the sisterhood and brotherhood

Joining the Prophetic Liberation Army as Revolutionists

Going to war against
The father-missing world

Going to war against
Lack of consciousness

Going to war against
Permanent Insanity

Armed with capable
Intervening soothing **words**

Armed with capable
Potent healing **lines**

Armed with capable
Foundation-building **phrases**

Armed with capable
Humanity-salvaging **thoughts**

Representing lost and dead souls
Predicted and found in

Dead Sea Scrolls
Fighting to become reborn

Flesh of Her flesh and
Seed of Her seed
Devour this whole rhyme
Or even a morsel of one line
Of my dying flesh
Feed off of it and
Become nourished by it
That you may grow strong
Continue the struggle
Live on and
Fight to **Be**
Come Re
Born

BONUS ALERT #1 (within this book only)

Jonny T the Poetical Prophet,

I love you man for keeping me in this music business for the last few decades, but I love you even more for forcing me to pursue my writing interests beyond a simple hobby or complicated score. Thanks for tirelessly pushing me hard to continue in this artistic expression. Even though we've long gone our separate ways, you were there from the start so you'll still be there in the excavated recesses of my heart!

One Love Rock On,
NKB

FUNK-NASTYFIED CHANGES
FOR JONNY T

Are you a reason, a season, or a fu**ing lifetime?
Think they are all the same?
You out your da** mind
Working with feelings and displaced memories
Got your mind left
Alternative solutions and potential solutions are
Fully laid to rest without peaceful civil unrest
R.I.P. Brother Ray, Rick James, independent news and
Relevant truths
Even V.I.P. man in the mirror reigning King of Pop
Couldn't shake loose the noose
Of the often just them legalized criminal system
While pure Haves force Have Nots to
Insure it's permanently us against them
Exposing the terrorists threats democracy across
The entire da** globe world
While supremely blind-eyeballing
The international dictator regime close at home
Becktel, Enron and the New World Order Bush Clan
Done did more dirt in less time
Than the combined AmeriKKKa's Most Wanted fam
Still majoring in minors jiving incomplete theories?
It's past time
Where you at?
Grab yo gat and secure
A reason, a season or
A fu**ing lifetime?

8. While we dine on fine vintage wine and
   Blackened salmon plate with cheesecake for
   desert and recount like a final back-page op.
   ed. piece subtitle
   The blackened death toll
   On our cheesy, guilt-ridden vintage hands

Precious Reader,

Life's most convincing obstacle and most tragic irony, is its inability to confront the issue of not seeking, and proudly claiming our own value and self-worth. We have absolutely nothing to prove to anyone else, yet positively everything to prove to ourselves. We frantically and hysterically attempt to please others, without taking care of home base first. Don't suffocate, castrate or amputate the curious creative and gloriously brilliant "inquisitive child" buried within (Especially not at the cheapened exchange rate of our immoral, bankrupt, unethical inhumane and insane current reality and global society). Fu** court, I stand in contempt of the Wars without End, that were launched not in our name, without any evidence, or trace of weapons of mass destruction or exit strategy. This antiquated piece was composed on the initial anniversary year of a war that would set precedence and impotence of the Geneva Convention, and any other false fragment of civilized nations and humanitarian progress.

Seated at the Right Hand

The Death Toll in Iraq
Done Cleared a hundred thousand
done cleared a Hundred Thousand
In brief, the commander in chief is a thief
And it is evident
Pre-emptative war, weapons of mass destruction, Iraq Freedom &
UN Charters are jumbled up empty theories of irrelevance
I'm heaven sent
Cause I bent the lens
So you can comprehend
And understand the sh** I spit

The Death Toll in Iraq
Done Cleared a hundred thousand
done cleared a Hundred Thousand
The conceived need
And perpetual greed
Still trying to justify the means
I mean we have seen
100,000 lives, murdered legalized torture and more brutality
In the last 3-6-5 than the combined reign
Of *Hussein, Mobutu, Kaddafi* and *Idi-Amin*
By the *American Bush Regime*

Democracy has brought Iraq an 85% unemployment rate,
100% privatization rate &
Ideas hypothetical
For rebuilding mosques, schools, libraries and
Human development

The Death Toll in Iraq
Done Cleared a hundred thousand
done cleared a Hundred Thousand
Cleared one hundred-thousands
Ten ten thousands
Ten thousand tens

What a disgrace and waste
When your faiths been erased and replaced
With FOX, CSPAN, and CNN
What a disgrace and waste when your faiths been erased
and replaced with fox, cspan and cnn
Luckily NPR, BBC, Telemundo and KPFK.org will broadcast live
G.W. and the Klan
Seated at the right hand
G.W. and the Klan Seated at the right hand
Not of God the Father, but the right hand of Sa-tan
From ingrate grand pops, pops
Even Laura and the Bushy Bushy twins turning tricks
Will still be practicing
Will still be practicing counting from 1 to 100,000
In Arabic

The Death Toll in Iraq
Done Cleared a hundred thousand
Done cleared a Hundred Thousand

9. All I have in this world is
   1 developing delicate love
   To redirect me
   From homicidal rage or suicidal depression,
   But . . .

Precious Reader,

This is my actual accounting and living testimony to my own truth. No matter where I go or what I do, I can't forget where I came from, why I'm here or where exactly I am going. There are only a mere handful of tangibles that no person can truly ever steal from you. You alone are always capable of recklessly squandering, forfeiting, giving away or negligently losing everything by your intentional choices or contradictions, and unintended outcomes and consequences.

LESS THAN I EVER WANTED

ALL I have in this world are (**4**)
Unsolved unaccounted for **strikes**
To help you hear me when I say feel me, but . . .

ALL I have in this world are (**4**)
Miniscule monumental **degrees**
To help you feel me when I say hear me, but . . .

ALL I have in this world are (**3**)
Priceless precious **children**
To represent me
When you misunderstand my thoughts and actions, but . . .

ALL I have in this world are (**2**)
Prestigious potent **nuts**
To help you evaluate your position
As I elevate my power preposition, but . . .

ALL I have in this world is (**1**)
Highly impacted heavy **sack**
To help bear my cross and pleasure burden, but . . .

ALL I have in this world is (**1**)
Magnified mesmerizing **word**
To help you decipher my concrete imagination, but . . .

ALL I have in this world is (**1**)
Developing delicate **love**
To redirect me from homicidal rage and suicidal depression, but . . .

ALL I have in this world is (**1**)
Limited longing **life**
To leave footprints of my beliefs, intentions, creations and impact, but . . .

One Tongue, One Love, One Life

ALL I have in this world is **(1)**
Suffocating sub-minimal **chance**
To convince high-class bourgeoisie minorities and
Lowlife illiterate rednecks
That I have just as much right as any to breath
Free air in this "great country of ours", but . . .

ALL I have in this world are **(0)**
Resilient realistic **opportunities**
To be young, gifted and black
And coexist peacefully in longevity
With those of limited experience, information, imagination,
Patience, tolerance or understanding, but . . .

ALL I have in this world are **(0)**
Ethical estranged **warnings or explanations**
Of the relevance of
Innocent until proven guilty, cruel and unusual punishment,
Justifiable homicide or wrongful death, but . . .

ALL I have in this world are **(0)**
Calculated or concealed **regrets**
Of anything that has been said or done
In the light or dark returning for an explanation, and

Lucky enough for this world of abuse, neglect and denial
The TOTALITY of my possessions is
Much **LESS** than I **EVER**
wanted
And
Much **MORE** than I **NEVER**
needed

BONUS ALERT #2 (wait there's more within this book only)

Erin,

Even though we only met to collaborate twice, I hope you are still handling your business in this game. Unfortunately when we shared selves, you still had to hit rock bottom before you could recognize the genuine compassion, concern and value of our contributions. You still have that triple edged sword of being beautiful, talented and confident. Unfortunately this business exposes that instead of reinforcing that. When the fork in the road entraps you, continue to be that strong stable surviving woman warrior until you return back to the sanctity of my wild concrete imagination, anxious fluid utensils and desperately patient vacant sheets.

One Love Rock On,
NKB

Funk-Nastyfied Nervous Laughter for Erin Powers

The **Powers** that you bestow on me don't need explaining
So the shadows of these spoken words are molded from the right
earlobe of you, **Erin**
Knowing it's the awkward nervous laughter
That got you hearing
Which masks my transparent insecurities, doubts and fears
I'm wearing
Which muzzles the overbearing sinful soul silent apologies
I'm blaring
Which blinds your translucent angelic internal radiance
I'm staring
Which numbs this radiating Congolese Passion heart of mine
I'm smearing
Cause, the confidentials of your core are treasures
Buried deep within
Pardon me, but
The departing invitations of the
Central volcanic eruptions of the diamond oil wells region parting
of your bare naked blanketed foreskin
Each sacred pilgrimage, death and fountain of youth revival
Since I entered and basked in
The Familiar of your Temple
Converts me to discipling and reminiscing

Hear stand I dread-locked and dead-locked in
This dreadful "Mr. Pitiful" condition
My own choice of violated trusts, sabotaged dreams and
Stolen aspirations got me wishing
I'd never been initially conceived or
Empowered to labor and deliver grief ever again

By sacrificing a loving stable home for
Homeless lust-filled indiscretions
In the stead of joy, peace, hope and laughter
Rooted in centuries of yearning and caring
I stand
Accused
I stand
Convicted
I stand
Accused and convicted by
The haunting present echoes
By the haunting present echoes (echoes, echoes) of the
Nervous laughter
The nervous laughter I'm
Still smearing
The nervous laughter I'm
Still hearing
The nervous laughter I'm
Still wearing
The nervous laughter I'm
Still sharing with you
Erin

10. Silencio como, an innocent victims
piercing hopes por
Justicia *(Justice)*
Silencio como, a serial killers
piercing haunting prayers por
Salvacion Eterna *(Eternal Salvation)*

Precious Reader,

This bilingual piece is dedicated to all the marginalized minorities who are truly making up globalized international majorities. Ironically, we are so preoccupied with other minorities and access to limited resources and constricted opportunities that we don't even pause to realize we merge and share a common oppressor and convoluted deliberate system of advanced, sophisticated and opportunistic oppression. Hence, a bilingual poem for multilingual people, countries and nations that even monolingual aware humans with open minds, courage and discipline will be able to respectfully translate and comprehend the universal themes and messages.

No Se Ch**ga con a Still-Born Infant's Piercing Demands por Representacion

En Augusto, I was reinvading distant relatives
En un pueblito muy olvidado
De Zacatecas, Mexico
To participate
En Mi Vida Loca

I had already been in the mix
Como cinco dias
Like an unofficially recognized mayor
Del pueblo porque
Hastaz las preciosas viejitas
Con bountiful pepper braids
Containing illusions y evidencias
De unfound purpose y unsolved mysteries
Would come out of their colorful cozy casitas
Para mirar me

Mientras
The innocent eternally grateful ninos
Would want to walk side-by-side con migo
A un camino
Desnivelado, lodoso
Sin pavementar porque en el ojo
Of their minds eye
Was identified as Jesus Christ myself
And La Virgin de Guadalupe
Was my holy virgin Madre

Early Sunday morning en el ultimo
Dia de mi momento
Mis sobrinas y sobrinos
Y their new found friends ranging from 9 to 13 anos
Were escorting me to the down-low ghetto hook up
Para compra huaraches
Of the finest leather
En una casa misteriosa
Como de curandera

I bought the dopest garments my feet
Had ever had the pleasure of being enclothed in

We began walking back
Through la plaza central cuando
Un viejito borracho anuncio
"PIN**E MAYATA"

Instinctamente, I stop
Distinctamente, I look around
Anciosemente, I wait
Pacientemente, I listen
And hear nada
Nada pero distant church bells ringing
And near song birds chirping

So then I eagerly fires back
Con energia
"Quien dice y que quieres
Porque si
Soy mayate
BUT I am puro ch**gon tambien"
Y la plaza entera esta ba en un
Silencio

Silencio como a mute lepper's
Piercing screams por
Reconocimento (recognition)

Silencio como a stillborn infant's
Piercing demands por
Representacion (representation)

Silencio como an innocent victim's
Piercing hopes por
Justicia (justice)

Silencio como a serial killer's
Piercing haunting prayers por
Salvacion Eterna (eternal salvation)

Silencio

Silencio until the engulfing laughter
De los Viejo's companeros de tequila
Echoed throughout the courtyard
Then we knew que
They knew que
I knew que
He knew que

A traves de todos the lands, y
A treves de todos the tongues, y
A traves de todos the times

No se ch**ga con al que le llaman
Double Duty
Porque I'm the wrong ni**a to funk with, y

No se ch**ga con al que le llaman
The Afrikanized Funk Nasty
Porque I'm the wrong ni**a to funk with, y

No se ch**ga con al que le llaman
Up From the Roots,
Porque that's the wrong band to funk with, y

Mijo, por favor
No se ch**ga con al que le llaman
El mui Ch**gon, P**chi Diablo, B**dejo
Buracho, C**rone, Negrito M**ate
Because
Soy
El MAS
Ch**gon

11. If the nappy synapsly
    Connected extensions of your soul
    Can't
    Move me,
    The arthritis in your cerebrum and
    Paralysis in your gonads
    Won't
    Move me

Precious Reader,

This piece is intended as a plea in the wilderness to return to the basic elements of our craft. A simple recognition and reminder that we need to elevate the standard and respect the work of poets who came before us. A request to actively resist the urge to become drunk and inflated with ourselves, our accomplishments (or lack of), our vision (or lack of), our innovation (or lack of) our commitment and multiple sacrifices (or lack of). Instead of a blatant disregard and disrespect, my prayer is that it is validated as a cry to the return of our ways and means in connection with our ultimate professional potential. As a guiding rubric, this is how I primarily measure my artistic endeavors, under the disguise of my undoubtedly harshest critic, myself.

This piece wasn't initially intended to burn bridges, hurt feelings or deflate egos. But if it serves as the springboard in order to secure a higher plateau of artistic innovation and professionalism, as a truth-teller then so be it!

SEE, YOU STILL AIN'T MOVED

If your **divine style**
Can't move me,
Your satanic imitation
Won't move me

If your **original creation**
Can't move me,
Your recycled replication
Won't move me

If your **infinitely potential mind**
Can't move me,
Oh no, Your retarded slow mo
Floor shows for sure
Won't move me

If your **lyrical content**
Can't move me,
Your ransom note holding the
Cold mic and hot stage hostage
Won't move me

If your **captive internal presence**
Can't move me,
Your attractive external appearance
Won't move me

If your **conceptually imaginative lines**
Can't move me,
Your inept capitalization & punctuation
Won't move me

If your **accurate visual word play**
Can't move me,
Your grammatically & politically correct diction and usage
Won't move me

If the **multiple meanings and contexts**
Of your phrases
Can't move me,
The single dimensions, definitions, translations and explanations
Won't move me

If the **nappy synapsly**
Connected extensions of your soul
Can't move me
Your agent and publicist's
Proven ability to misspell
Unprofessional, Disgraceful,
Repulsive, Whack & Horr-i-ble
Won't move me

If the **combination of these gestures**
Can't move you to move me
If the combination of these gestures
Can't move you
To move me

Your stymied utterances and
Discombobulated placements
Inviting complete fragments &
Incomplete phrases
To test my patience and For
Giving grace to allow you to continue
Displaying disrespect for the art form and
Complete disregard to the
Blatant proof that

You still ain't moved, you
Still ain't moved, still
Ain't moved, ain't
Moved
MOVED

I *look into your soul* and
see, You still ain't moved
I *feel the reaction* of the audience and
see, You still ain't moved
I *smell the grotesque stench* of disappointment and
see, You still ain't moved
I *taste the audacity* of your despair and
see, You still ain't moved
I *hear the cleansing vomit* of pioneering and enduring poets and
see, You still ain't moved

The **common senses** of
These five **complete senses**
Still ain't brought you **back to your senses**
Cause **I senses**

You still ain't moved
So fu** *applause*, fu** *ovation*, fu**
Recognition, fu***peace* and fu** *see you later*
Cause, see
You still ain't moved
Still ain't moved
Ain't moved
Moved

Moved you, moved me
Moved them, moved we
Moved skills, moved ability
Moved imagination, moved creativity
Moved spoken word, moved poetry
Moved willingly, moved gracefully
Moved cautiously, moved respectfully
Moved responsibly, moved progressively
Moved authentically, moved reflectively
Moved continually, moved eventually
Moved, moved, moved
period

12. While most misprioritized disorganized men
    Are busy chasing & eating green-berets
    For breakfast

    Baby you know
    NK Bwana's
    Just patiently
    Holding steadfast

Precious Reader,

I would not traditionally exhibit this particular piece as a model of my finest work. However, I dare exhibit this piece as a witnessed model of my own frailty, humanity and courageous risk-taking. We all must actively confront and engage with these occasional dilemmas, in order to grapple with our own comfort zones, develop our own tolerance, patience, hearing, understanding and objectivity while literally destroying false barriers and expanding self-prescribed horizons. So I stand bare before you with nothing but purpose and courage to protect me. Fortunately, courage is all anyone needs. Without courage, no other virtues exist.

I HUNGER 4 THEE

I hunger 4 Thee
Cause see **Lady**
I hunger 4 Thee

Mi Mama always told me
Come te primero
Y jugas te segundo
Meaning eat first and play second

I hunger 4 Thee
Cause see **Maybe**
I hunger 4 Thee

I've always taken her advice
All my life
And while most
Misprioritized disorganized men
Are busy chasing & eating green berets
For breakfast
Baby you know
NK Bwana's just patiently
Holding steadfast

I hunger 4 Thee
Cause see **Baby**
I hunger 4 Thee

Since
My souls
Sole surmountable chance

At **primarily**, nibbling all
Your playful hourderves

At **continually**, consuming all
Your bountiful spread nerves

At **climaxingly**, ejaculating all
Your screaming creaming joyful desert

I **hunger** 4 Thee
Cause see Lady
Cause see Maybe
Cause see Baby
I hunger 4
Thee

13. Sure to lead to the eventual collapse and relapse
    To corresponding memories
    Of the collisions and connections that

    Recreated courage
    In your concrete nipples

    Recycled joy
    In every nook and crevice
    Of your constricting vaginal walls

    Rejuvenated piece
    In your cautious cheekbones

    Revived hope
    In your convincing smile, and

    Recessitated purpose
    In your conspicuous eyes

Precious Reader,

I predict that most readers and active listeners already think this unique delicate piece is especially just for all the fine women and ladies. You are only partially correct. The truth of the matter is that this piece is my attempt in trying to speak to the masses of hopeful distant lovers who have experienced that single timeless moment when you have tried to express the single sentiment of elation that someone provokes and completely exhaust your storage vault of diction and action. Instead of abruptly aborting, making a U-turn or just frustratingly attempting to ignore it (waiting in vain for your love); it is my desire that maybe a morsel in this piece may compel you to push forward and keep pursuing attempts to communicate.

COME, AS I DO (YOU)

Come to me
When your cognition correctly confirms
That your concrete consciousness contemplates
Compatible communication currents

Come to me
When the critical and confusing confirmations
Of these compatible communication currents
Conversely and complexly convene
And convert beyond conventional intimate conversations,
Communications and contemplations

Come to me
When concurrent converted common cordial correspondence
Cohabitate, coerce combat and combine
To confidently confirm
Congruent correlations between
Will, time, space, fears and opportunities

Come to me
When you are not confused
Or conditionally capped and categorized
Within your own experiences,
Contaminatingly controlled
By your own fears and apprehensions,
Crucifyingly commanded
By the hope and trust of the potential and possibility
Of truth, freedom and justice

Come to m,
When you have considered the costs and consequences
Of loneliness and loss of hope and confidence
On your countenance &
Create conditions to compose and compress your contour
Containing concern and compassion
Commonly called a hug or clasp

Better yet an embrace so pure and powerful
It is capable of contrasting and contradicting
Real and imagined hurt, pain, negativity, abuse and neglect
While continually constructing and contributing to conditions
Composed of character, composure, and confidence
Capable of converting your position
On the possibility of pure love at the decaying core

Come with me
As we couple to codify and
Clarify visions, dreams, ambitions and apprehensions

Come with me
As we combine with confidence to
Confess complex configurations of
Power, grace, mercy, justice and beauty
That are confined and conditionally controlled
In your concealed creative limitations and intentions

Come with me
As we contemplate with caution
Sharing all that we presently contain in every context
Continually conveying concepts and
Combinations to reach prospects
While courageously climbing and continuing
Through the peaks, valleys, waterfalls and quicksand's
Of life

Come for me
As I carnally and compulsively
Gargle your cockle commodity
Convincingly communicating with the conjunction junction
Of your goddess function

Come for me
As my Congolese-Passion
Concealed in my co**
Tails your cocktail
Communally coerced, convinced and connected
By your collarbone and my pelvic bone create captive cohesion
And clear compression, suspension and expression
Of the appropriately complex combination
Of calculated strategic fu**ing
Balanced with compassionate intimate love-making

Come for me
As I commentate, compliment and cater
To the needs of your comestible content
And complicated components
That constitute your cosmic constellation and
Considerately clutch your cuticles
As the coalition and coercion of your vaginal
Vibrations and my sensitive testicle tentacles
Coerce me into the sweetest death
With your colander as my coffin
Without coughing

Come for me
As you critically clasp my clavicle
As I cloak, clog, clobber and
Crush the emptiness in your soul
With the completeness of my semen

Come for me
As the carefree combination and combustion
Causes cardiac convulsions
Cosmic seismic vibrations
Carnivorous and barbarous behaviors

That are sure to lead to the eventual collapse and relapse
To corresponding memories of the collisions and connections
That recreated courage
In your concrete nipples
Recycled joy
In every nook and crevice of your constricting vaginal walls
Rejuvenated peace
In your cautious cheekbones
Revived hope
In your convincing smile and
Recessitated purpose
In your conspicuous eyes

Comfort me
As we consummate the communion and
Conform to the true peace, love and joy that
Passes and surpasses understanding and cocaine

Comfort me
As we continue to cohabitate cooperatively
Collaboratively and continually
Convincingly completing expressions
Of passion, compassion, grace and mercy

Comfort me
As we courageously volunteer
To be colonized by love instead of fear
In body, mind and spirit

Comfort me
As we commit and commemorate the composition
Of sacredness and sanctity of the communion
Of companions
In compassion

Comfort me
As you consume me
Like a true connoisseur of quality
Savoring the uniqueness and unity
Of desire and maintenance in tranquility

Comfort me
As I continually convoke and invoke
My elders, elders, elders
To coordinate efforts
To concretely correspond, consequently congratulate and
Courageously convince them
That I comprehend and
Clearly unconditionally express

Love does, Love is and
Love always will be
From before their time
And beyond ever since
Habitually continuing and celebrating
Their combined legacy

Comfort me
As I conclude these sentiments
I confess
My unconditional love for you and the witness
I bear to the evidence
Of the completeness
Of your infinite legacy and unyielding essence

I pray that before your moment
You will witness what I witness
In your presence
And in your absence

Come *to* me
Come *with* me
Come *for* me, and
Comfort me,
As "**I do**" You

BONUS ALERT #3 (but wait there's even more, for a limited time for the first million customers we'll throw in within this book only . . ."

Frank Turner,

First of all, congratulations on a smashing fourth album (with an easily anticipated four more to go before the greatest hits millennium C.D.)! It is purely remarkable how this music and art thing connects the entire globe beyond the intergalactic universal digital citizenry. We are truly twin-lineal brothers from other mothers. Until the Wessex boy or the Congolese boy reunite in Whembley, Canada, The Virgin Islands or the Glass House in Pomona, everyone can still pour a glass and sing. Or merely, grab my flask and don't look back until our hearts, homes and histories find common courses to reunite like two bucket list rusted coffee cans just having fun from the rivers leading to British Seas along the familiar passage back from the West Nile River banks.

Cheers Mate one Love and Rock On!
NKB

Funk-Nastyfied England, Keep My Bones

Frank Turner Tribute

Before this *Wessex Boy* writes his own fu**ing *Eulogy*
I'm gonna keep *One Foot Before the Other* until *I am Disappeared*
Forsaking *Glory Hallelujah* while trying to break this *English Curse*
Even though *Peggy Sang the Blues* while *I Still Believe*
every line in every verse
Truly yours *England keep my bone, If Ever I Stray*
"*At least I fu**ing tried*" seeking *Redemption* and crossing still *Rivers*
Before final *Nights Become Days*

14. I'm one in a million

Courageous warrior, buffalo soldiers and
Countless forgotten others
Who receive more purple hearts and medals of
honor
Overseas

Than the hearts anguish and dishonor of
Overseeing the mettling in the real business
Of this forsaken country

Precious Reader,

We have so much digital access at our fingertips. It appears that the more we have advanced, the more we have regressed. In terms of respect for our retrospective past experiences, struggles and boundless successes we are still regressing. It is a blessing and a curse. We fail to remember what our ancestors, foremothers and forefathers sacrificed in order to blaze a trail. They couldn't even conceive what we currently yield. We collectively repay them with oblivious disregard and blatant disdain. They surely must be rolling in their graves watching us flush hard won freedoms and responsibilities down the toilet. This piece is my humble redemptive tithe to convey I still remember and I still believe.

ONE IN A MILLION TARNISHED EYES & SAPPHIRE KNUCKLES

I'm **one in a million**
Crooked teeth busted in
When you are trying to starve yourself to death
Refusing to eat
On a foreign slave ship named
"The Heart of Jesus"

I'm **one in a million**
Missing lineage links
In the faces at the bottom of the vaults
Of the triangular trade route Trans-Atlantic

I'm **one in a million**
Million well fed fish
Feasting on the bone marrow
Of decapitated tomorrows and indefinable sorrow
Hidden sentiments
In the camouflaged sediment
In the crust at the base of the ocean floor

I'm **one in a million**
Lashes in the exposed resistance and
Decomposed back and flesh
Ob dat ignant fiel ni**a
Who ain't tryin to git it
When that well kept house nigger
Vainly explains
What the masters used clothes, overseeing duties
Country Time lemonade
And motherfu**ing shade
Was all about

I'm *one in a million*
Pre-destined fates
Of a million forced rapes
Occurring on a million unsolicited dates
In a million strange ways
On a million infamous times
In a million impregnated minds
Time after time, night after night
Decade after decade and century after century
So there we have been
Cause here we now are

I'm *one in a million*
Courageous warriors, buffalo soldiers and
Countless forgotten others
Who receive more purple hearts and medals of honor overseas
Than the hearts anguish and dishonor of
Overseeing the mettling in the real business
Of this forsaken country
While our hearts, breasts and chests
Are savagely ripped open
Revealing the tarnished eyes, sapphire knuckles and
Still faintly beating violet hearts
In our home country

I'm *one in a million*
Sweet sable mothers
And ebony families having to contact coroners
Mortuaries while arranging obituaries
And delivering eulogies
Because another lustrous luminous
Light was extinguished before their own dawn

Prematurely before childhood had officially ended and
Adulthood narrowly begun
At the hands of yet another one
With a rusty knife, police baton
Or stolen gun

Just an entire almanac unfold (Loved one)
Just a complete volume untold (loved One)
Just a total hymnbook unsung (LOVED one)
Just an enchanted secret garden unsprung (loved ONE)

I'm **one in a million**
Nameless, faceless prisoners of war
Or more realistic, accurate and correct
Prisoners of class and race
Doing life behind bars, or
Doing scars behind life
I serve your time
With these bleeding pens, fading scripts
And occasionally with this black box, dim lights and mic

I'm the wisdom delivering
Ash follicles to your escalated years
I'm the shoulder blade delivering
Renewing sustenance to your pleading tears
I'm the wind chime delivering
Youthful character to your laugh lines & toothless grins

I'm **one in a million**
Resounding hearts pounding
To that redundantly obvious rhythm
Of those repugnant familiar blues
Till Jesus, Doubting Thomas, Mother Theresa, Gandhi
Princess Di and fu** it
Even Elvis will have to join in

I'm *one in a million*
Extended discernable lines and bars
Of Phyllis Wheatley's first published poem

I'm *one in a million*
Smoldering homes and Negro churches
The scientific method infused in the encoded carbon 14
Of the four little black school girls
Incinerated and desecrated
In the sanctuary of their Sunday School room world

I'm *one in a million*
Mass grave sites and undiscovered
Shallow tombs

I'm *one in a million*
Million voices
Making conscious choices
Still waiting to overcome someday
While hesitating and realistically expecting
Some more devastating
Understated news today

I'm *one in a million*
Stubbornly rooted branches
From the maple, cedar and oak
That our grand pops and great grand pops
Would have swung from till their neck popped
All for
An alleged look

I'm *one in a million*
Unsuccessful sadistic racist abortions
That still matured till full term

I'm *one in a million*
Reasons that even though seasons change
There are no temporary fixes or solutions
To a race problem that is convoluted
And perm-a-nent
Tell the president, I said it
And I have always meant it

I'm *one in a million*
Great great-granddaughters and
Not so great great-grandsons
Of Frederick Douglass, Sojourner Truth and John Brown
Who will turn this world around
Turn this mess upside down
Guaranteed to bring hell into town
Until we discontinue the abandonment and
Continue where previous abolitionist went

I'm *one in a million*
Ghetto smiles disguising
Rebellious militants uprising
Broken word truth-tellers reminding

So you can march on Washington or the mountain go tell it
You can march on Washington or the mountain go tell it son
Baldwin, Mandela, Malcolm, Martin and Farrakhan have previously
solved the sum

That 1 plus 1 plus 1 in a strong million
Like rats, roaches and ants
Won't stop loving, won't stop laughing, won't stop living
Won't stop trying, won't stop fighting, won't stop dying
Until the task is completed and the job is well done
The task completed and job well done

I'm *one in a million*
Miracles still holding on
Miracles still staying strong
Miracles still moving on

Miracles still right black where I **Be Come**
Still right black where I **Be From**
Still right black where I **Be Home**
Still right black where I **Be Long**

15. Yes, I am Being
    Yes, I am Becoming
    Yes, I will Become and
    Yes, I Can

Precious Reader,

I have finally learned through much wasted time, energy and effort that when someone informs me that they were "shocked, pleasantly surprised or absolutely had no idea that I could blah, blah, blah" it isn't really an acknowledgment of me. It's a virtual apology for the assumption or prejudice they placed on themselves. I've grown not to even sweat it or give it a second thought. There is no need to defend or respond to apologies of lack of awareness or newfound insight or perspective. Instead, not only am I able, this is probably the least I can do. As a matter of fact, I'm continuously challenging myself, learning, improving and developing into a sharper, crisper and more complete me. If you don't keep growing, you are already dead.

One Tongue, One Love, One Life

Yes I am, Yes I Can

Sometimes life just hands you
A whole bunch of no's

No
No money, no family, no friends
No mentors, no opportunities

No
No money, no homes, no food
No clothes, no opportunities

No
No money, no education, no books
No homework, no opportunities

No
No money, no job, no credit
No checks, no opportunities

Never G-I-V-E U-P and
Keep your H-E-A-D U-P
Never G-I-V-E U-P and
Keep your H-E-A-D U-P
Never G-I-V-E U-P and
Keep your H-E-A-D
U-P

Sometimes life just hands you
A whole bunch of maybe's

Maybe
Somehow, someway, someday
You'll have an idea

Maybe
Somehow, someway, someday
You'll have an opportunity

Maybe
Somehow, someway, someday
You'll still continue to dream

Maybe
Somehow, someway, someday
You'll become somebody

Never G-I-V-E U-P and
Keep your H-E-A-D U-P
Never G-I-V-E U-P and
Keep your H-E-A-D U-P
Never G-I-V-E U-P and
Keep your H-E-A-D
U-P

Sometimes you just
Have to turn it all around and
Hand life back a whole bunch of yes's

Yes
I am somebody and
Yes, I can

Yes
I am unique and worthwhile and
Yes, I can

Yes
I have good ideas and bad ideas and
Yes, I can

Yes
I make mistakes and learn from my mistakes and
Yes, I can

Yes
I can and will help you and
Yes, I can

Yes
I do love you and I do love myself and
Yes, I can

Yes
I will always keep my head up and never give up and
Yes, I can

Yes
I am being
Yes
I am becoming
Yes
I will become and
Yes, I can

Yes
I am and
Yes, I can

Yes
I AM and
Yes, I CAN

Yes I am, and
Yes I can

Never G-I-V-E U-P and
Keep your H-E-A-D U-P
Never G-I-V-E U-P and
Keep your H-E-A-D U-P
Never G-I-V-E U-P and
Keep your H-E-A-D
U-P

Yes, I am
Yes, I can
Yes, Yes
Yes!!!

16. Genociding your initial instincts
    Leaving you sensing
    My thoughts flow like
    Flushed sweating piss
    Cumming out of my penis

DIVINE STYLE VS. DEMONIC WORD PLAY A FUNK NASTY SPELL

Precious Reader,

The original purpose of my quick write exercises are to awaken the creative demons and allow organic thoughts to transform from can't get right stalemates to just write it baby stages. Apparently, there was a strong current or correlation with the entire juices and flowing theme. I would offer an apology in advance, but truthfully I write poems for myself and elect to share them with others. There are times however, that I continue to harbor feelings of frustration and irritation when I'm misconstrued, misunderstood or under appreciated. Others can only slow you down or bring you down temporarily, only you have the power and ability to make it permanent. Respect talents, respect gifts, respect artists and the creative processes they embark on while maintaining purpose and self-respect.

THOUGHTS FLOW LIKE PISS

Don't prey
Pray to visualizing
Under false pretense or

Prey
Pray to criticizing
My developing thesis or

Prey
Pray to jeopardizing
My poetic license or

Prey
Pray to genociding
Your initial instincts

Leaving you sensing
My thoughts flow
Like flushed sweating piss
Gushing out of my penis

My abstract linguist jizzim
Combustion is the meanest

Come now truly
Have you seen this?

God-given talent
Display correspondence
Of blatant latent
Kinetic creative genius

17. While you still contesting
    Desperately spitting and
    Trying to pass on
    Inconsistent shallow concepts in
    Got-no-tone
    Disguised as
    Mo-no-tone

Precious Reader,

This particular piece is an ironic exercise in judgment, mercy, humility and mind control. It's mind control when an uninvited loud-mouth, no sense-making, breath-stinking, stranger, imitation poet or writer bombards me with their unsolicited opinion about my existence, craft or body of work. It's mind control because I do not say it, but I am strategically internally thinking it loud and clear. If it were polite or correct I would take the pillow from their head and slap a book in it.

MISFITS OF THE CRACKED, CHAPPED, DRY LIPS

Your sh** is
Dry

Your sh** is
Drier than
Starched Stone Mountain southern-bred
Crackers
Eating extra seasoned saltine Planters crackers
In the central high noon summer sun rays at
The center of the Sahara Dessert

You sh** is
Drier than
Extracting the last mirage of
Moisture from your decrepit, bleeding
Decomposing lips—chapped
Meditating on wished soothing relief found in
Fingertip jars of flavored stick-chap

Your sh** is
Dry and incarcerated
With throat lacerating
Suffocating on the razor blade of
Hollow crackling straw ain't working
And you're out back in the outback
Off jerking off
On your rawest original stolen poem

Better yet imitation interpretation
Irish Limerick
Of invisible existence
And illiterate lyrics
Impersonating greatest hits of
Justin Timberlake, Buddy Holly
And oh yes Elvis

Your sh** is
Dry and while you still contesting
Desperately spitting and
Trying to pass on
Inconsistent shallow concepts in
Got-No-tone
Disguised as
Mo-No-tone

I know I've already
Dedicated far too many seconds
To attempt to align
With the Spoken Word time
your attention deficit disorder a**

So without further mention or
Attempt to hold my patience and aggression
In detention
Please allow me to pass

And get my proud, narrow black a**
To my next paid
Speaking engagement session
Without your arid, stale, pale, salty
Crusty, musty, jealous zealous
A**

18. Oh sh**, No sh**
    That sh** used to be hip hop truest piece
    Of the revolution come
    Fu** the norm
    Sacred art form
    Of Peace
    That every worldwide ghetto we know
    From the O-town to Chicago
    Tokyo to Soweto
    Had on lock
    Up in this piece

Precious Reader,

At this point I anticipate that I have provided sufficient evidence that I am always attempting to distinguish myself from the generic mediocrity-infested pack. I believe that we are entering a new dawn that has the potential to retrieve us from the abyss of mediocrity and sludge that passes for art without craft, rhyme without reason, dialogue without understanding, function without purpose, and familiarity without passion. We need to step back and take a cleansing healing look at ourselves and our development with respect to art, music, hip-hop, poetry and all things written, read and spoken. What legacy are we leaving and what are we transmitting to current and future generations regarding our social and cultural values and priorities? How are each of our behaviors and actions aligned with these "professed" values and priorities? Join me in combatting the familiar with simplistic thought, increased genuine will, reinforced skill, and deliberate actions.

WHILE THOUGHTS LINGER

In this
Corrupt concrete jungle
I still hunger
Full of anger
While thoughts linger
While thoughts linger and get
Blasted out of my wandering thoughts of peace
By some overbearing, over-blaring barren
Creation that is a piece
Of sh**, no sh** that sh**
Used to be hip-hop's truest piece
Of the Revolution come
Fu** the norm
Purest sacred art form of peace
That every worldwide ghetto we know
From the O-town to Chicago, Tokyo to Soweto
Had on lock up in this piece

Now that 98.99% of hip-hop done flip-flopped
Done flip-flopped
98.99% of hip-hop done flip-flopped

Got less content (for rent)
Than that last death row dinner

Got less flow (for sure)
Than post menopause lesbian lovers

Got less beef (in their teeth)
Than vegans who don't perform sex oral

Got less show (you know)
Than confessing nothing wicked, sly or immoral

Got less credit (to spend kid)
Than black home loans in the middle of the Great Depression

Got less glow (hell no)
Than Ted Danson's lone black face impression

In this
Corrupt concrete jungle
I still hunger
Full of anger
While thoughts linger
While thoughts linger and get
Blasted out of my wandering thoughts of peace
By some overbearing, over-blaring barren
Creation that is a piece
Of sh**, no sh** that sh**
Used to be hip-hop's truest piece
Of the Revolution come
Fu** the norm
Purest sacred art form of peace
That every worldwide ghetto we know
From the O-town to Chicago, Tokyo to Soweto
Had on lock up in this piece

Since barely 1% of hip-hop ain' t flip-flopped
Ain't flip-flopped
Barely 1% of hip-hop ain't flip-flopped

Still got
More **real feel**
Than virgin corn-holes in the entire prison system

Still got
More **prophesy**
Than Phife Dog *Bustin a nut inside your eye to show you where he come from*

Still got
More **creativity**
Than *Uncle Ricky, could you tell me a bed time story please*

Still got
More **concrete**
Than tackle football on the block in street traffic no pads

Still got
More **destination**
Than Biggie, *Know what it's like to wake up fu**ed up, Pockets broke as hell another rock to sell, People look at you like you the loser, Selling drugs to all the users mad buddah abusers*

Still got
More **return**
Than x-Clan's, *Van glorious this is protected by the red, the black and the green at the crossroads with a key, sissy*

Still got
More **stability**
Than Sugar Hills, *To the hip hop, hip it to the hip, and you hip-hip the hop and don't stop the rock*

Still got
More **juice**
Than Pac hollering, *Without your word you a shell of a man, I lost respect for you ni**a we can never be friends, I know what's running through your head now, What would you do if it was up to you I'd be dead now, Let the world know you a coward you could never be live, Till I die see the motherfu**ing bi**h in your eyes, The type of ni**a let the evil of the money trap me so when you see me ni**a you better get at me*

That's that real ill-hype sh**
Hip-hop dope flow type sh**
That used to blast the space between wandering thoughts of peace
Till some overbearing, over-blaring barren creation that is a piece
Of sh**, no sh** that sh**
Used to be hip-hop's truest piece
Of the Revolution come, fu** the norm
Purest sacred art form of peace
That every worldwide ghetto we know
From the O-town to Chicago, Tokyo to Soweto
Had on lock up on this piece of
Corrupt concrete jungle,
I still hunger
Full of anger
While thoughts linger
While thoughts linger and still
Get
Blasted

19. Thou shalt not,
   Irresponsibly create an external scapegoat
   For the time with yourself
   You ain't spent

Precious Reader,

Excuse me for just having a downright fantastic time producing this "edutainment" piece. It is completely "edutainment" because I'm educating you (hopefully) as well as myself (possibly) with the real lofty supreme values. It is also "edutainment" because I'm also entertaining you (possibly) as well as myself (definitely) with the real low down dirty shame. I hope you enjoy it even half as much as I do, (but please don't stop there). Think about it, what would you cherish for yourself or your loved ones given complete control?

MY GET OUT OF HELL FREE CARD

Thou shalt not
Apprehensively strangle Mic's
Without gems of lyrical content

Thou shalt not
Steal copy written rhymes
When the space in your mind remains for rent

Thou shalt not
Arrogantly declare war
Without strategic fatality assessment

Thou shalt not
Cautiously enter the ring
Without immediate stamina supplement

Thou shalt not
Hopelessly battle a true Spoken Word poet
Without lethal resources potent

Thou shalt not
Display or just play yourself
Without completing anger management

Thou shalt not
Suicidally brandish burned burners
Without vigorous hollow-point bullets

Thou shalt not
Desperately call Jacoby & Meyers
When you run up, get done up, broke off and just bent

Thou shalt not
Mockingly disclose the gator wallet
Without sufficient monetary content

Thou shalt not
Boastfully claim cock-diesel
Without confirming final results for prostate cancer, colon cancer or
impotence

Thou shalt not
Deceitfully lie to the opposite sex
To create illusions of grandeur or importance

Thou shalt not
Disclose soiled panties
Without prior verbal confirmed agreement
10-4 good buddy, roger that

Thou shalt not
Regretfully separate moist luke-warm thighs
Without adequate available reinforcement

Thou shalt not
Authentically judge my life
Without evidence of good intent

Thou shalt not
Unexpectedly criticize my rhymes
Without prior informed consent

Thou shalt not
Consciously walk across the street
When you remember any of the dollars I lent

Thou shalt not
Devilishly sin 6 & ½ days, go to church ½ a day
And think you will escape punishment

Thou shalt not
Irresponsibly create a scapegoat
For the time with yourself you ain't spent

Thou shalt not
Completely alienate family and friends
When they're caught in a bad predicament

Thou shalt not
Wickedly convince God to tell me to
"Shut the fu** up"
When I attempt to use this
Extension of the Ten Commandments
As my
Get out of hell free card
Down Payment

20. How simply we erase, edit and rephrase
    Concurrent history
    To the cyclical redundant, period
    Where voicing atrocities and modern-day
    massacres mentally
    Masturbates and menstruates of
    Blasphemy

Precious Reader,

I am nauseated by our limited understanding and awareness of cultural histories and legacies that are intertwined with our own experiences and realities. It is insufficient to blame the schools and teachers for shallow depth or breadth of our confined awareness and understanding. As the digital age dominates the global capacities and latent potential that communication may yield, the monolingual, monoculture at are a gross disadvantage in competition or inclusion. Where better to begin in the alleged American Histories than the reminders we receive without even casually relating them to the current realities of indigenous nations, tribes, villages and peoples across the entire globe. Rather than pause to think globally we can't reenact locally the experiences of current Native Americans or indigenous tribal or nomadic people that are more concretely tied to the land and way of being than any simulated avatar experience could generate or potentially stimulate. Respect your own future, by honoring and revering their past and co-creating a better present relationship and reality.

HARBORED VESSELS OF CONTEMPT

Reservation—*an arrangement to have something held for one's use*

Breathless, lies the frail shell of
Alleged existence
Until continuously
Support to consciousness
Beneath the surface and
Between the lines
At birth separated twins to the t-shirt outlined
With "Got Land? Thank
An Indian"

Pause temporarily to rewind time and
Replace Thank an Indian
with an African, a Mexican, a Chinaman
or a Woman man

How simply we erase, edit and rephrase
Concurrent history
To the cyclical redundant, period
Where voicing atrocities and modern-day massacres mentally
Masturbates and menstruates of
Blasphemy
Even if we be P.C. and
Correctly pronounce Native American

Tried, tested and true American-made patriotic in
The halls of Winchester, Colt and Smith & Wesson
Banners spangled in stars

Harboring vessels of contempt for all strong occurring currents and
Reoccurring currents of resistance
Death-defying existence of
Ones once labeled as savages

Numeric representations of this nation's infatuation
With pagan arithmetic experimentation
And exponential long division of
Native Life expectancy averages
Within the collective human experiences
Of pre-right now decades
U.N. civilized nations still fail
Relevant civilized humanitarian lessons

Whose use is this normalized absurdity reserved for?
What have the truly yours land + culture whores
Offered in its stead
Except crumbs and loaves of suicide, alcoholism, drug addiction and
Poverty they've been fed
A paranoid Polaroid synopsis
Of anti-establishment antidepressants
Should have been discarded and dismissed centuries ago
As madness, myth, urban legend, myth and folklore

Most mis-informed, mis-educated, yet accurately-trained
Lower folk deny physical and psychological resilience
To Inter-Tribal, Vision Quests, Sweat Lodges and the power of the
Ancient Ways
Passed on to the strong
Through wisdom, prayers, praise offerings and sage
Modern day warriors
Combatting underlying rage
Through daily revival, renewed pride, unsurpassed honor and
Powerful pockets of spiritual resistance

Reservations of Nations
Past, present and future in hand
Demonstrate to atheists
The vitality of Ceremony

Reservations of Nations
Past, present and future in hand
Demonstrate to enemies of families
The necessity of Tribal Comradery

Reservations of Nations
Past, present and future in hand
Demonstrate to chaos and turmoil
The constancy of Peace

Reservations of Nations
Past, present and future in hand
On the shoulder blade of
Ancestors and totem poles tall stand

Beyond the confined boundaries
Openly exalting and fiercely reminding
"Got Land? Thank an Indian".

21. Just Move
   Send,
   Advanced notices of payment on delivery
   For past due grievances before slavery
   Justice, democracy and liberty
   Were erased terms and antonyms
   For just plain "ni**ery"
   Again

Precious Reader,

If you are still, you begin to recognize how the masses are lead like sheep to the slaughterhouse by such a rare imbalanced few. The majority of the coercion is voluntary and based on fear or loss. The entire psyche of deficit thinking or "not enough for everyone, I gotta get mine you gotta get yours" mentality has us entrapped into a vicious cycle of poverty, abandonment, hoarding, and schizophrenic paranoia. We need to boldly interrupt and log jam this cycle and replace it with pure thoughts, right living and most importantly deliberate actions. This piece is a humane reminder that is intended to be hot enough to charge and jumpstart the heart to boldly thaw out anything that prevents the capacity of your heart, brain and body to be compelled to actions. Only you know what your intimate needs are. Therefore, the answers to your temporary dilemmas and obstacles reside within you as well. Set them free and just move!

MIDWIFING MOVEMENTS

Just move, just move, just move, just move
Just move, just move, just move, just move

Just Move
    When,
    The soul of resistance
    Creates right thoughts
    Controlled by right actions
    Again

Just Move
    Then,
    Shut your mouth up
    Let the evidence of your actions
    Be the only motion talking
    Again

Just Move
    Mend,
    Differences over ways and means
    And everything's trivial in between
    Again

Just Move
    Bend,
    Every physical rule
    Break every psychological tool
    Till every unlocking chain's
    Reacting
    Again

One Tongue, One Love, One Life

Just Move
> Send,
> Advanced notices of payment on delivery
> For past due grievances before slavery
> Justice, democracy and liberty
> Were erased terms and antonyms
> For just plain "ni**ery"
> Again

Just Move
> Friends,
> To prove their allegiance
> Examine our resistance, visualize our existence and
> Return to root
> Again

Just Move
> Stand,
> Up get up
> For your rights with
> Less lip-smacking for practice and
> More guns clapping on captains
> Again

Just Move
> In,
> Stride with
> Your conscience is your guide
> Especially while
> New new world order creating and
> Old old tomb raiding
> Again

Just Move
    And,
    Don't look back when
    Defective allies turn they back on what's right and
    Just merely keep on smiling and merrily, merrily, merrily, merrily
    We wear the mask Franz Fanon—emal acting
    Again

Just Move
    Spend,
    More time with old souls and genuine minds to
    Shape lives and Robin Hood wrong crimes and
    Change the course of what's happening
    Again

Just Move
    Kin,
    Regardless of race, sex, language, religion or origin
    In emotional, psychological physical and armed struggle continues
    We're all countrymen
    Till ashes to ashes, dust-to-dust bodies return
    But, spirits live on in
    Actions of warriors, comrades, buffalo soldiers and
    Proven friends
    Again

Just Move
    Ment,
    To remove not sooth
    Include not exclude
    Make moves not coincidentally pursue
    By incident nor accident
    Again

Just Move
> Women,
> To become better fathers
> Secure our spiritual past and
> Protect our psychological presence
> Well-balanced
> Again

Just Move
> Men,
> To become better mothers
> Abort limited visions, vested interests, and destructive egos then
> Give birth to
> Just societies and humane practices
> Again

Just Move, kin
Just Move, friends
Just Move, women
Just Move, men
Just Move,—ment
Just Move,—ment

Just move, just move, just move, just move
Just move, just move, just move, just move
Just move
Again and again and again
Or you'll look up and we'll have already been gone my friend

22. Her jaw locked on my finger
    I securely pried my knuckle out
    It wasn't until I saw the warm blood, milky
    fluid, and mucus
    Sea spray foam ooze from her nostrils and
    mouth
    That I distinctly understood
    What death's uncivilized patience were all about

Precious Reader,

This unique piece truly stretched me out as a poet and writer. I was torn and forced to write from another perspective while eliminating my senses as a father and keeper of my child under extreme duress. After this life-changing experience it is much easier to empathize with the countless mothers and families of death row inmates, terminal illness patients, or even hospice infants. It wasn't until I wore the envious glares of families at facilities like Children's Hospitals who only face one final way of leaving the facility indefinitely, instead of collectively as a complete family with only 24 hours of complete treatment care and observation. I was grateful that the Lord was merciful and gracious on that familiar night that my complacent life ended and my deliberate, purpose-driven, joyful service-leadership stewardship began.

Night That Simultaneously Beat Hearts (rewind time)

My eighteen-month old
Stopped breathing unexpectedly the other day
All of my unstated dreams and unfound hopes
Evaporated in the same way

It started with some faint
Continuous coughs
Disconnected distractions became focused
As her pleading gasps for air began to fall off

Her trembling shrieks of pain and fright
Were barely audible
The frozen grapes afternoon treat
Proved indigestible

Each frantic first aide blow to her chest and back
Beat stronger and stronger
Personally rebuking Lucifer, while
Death was motivated and valiantly lingered

I squeezed from her seven-pound belly
In desperate attempts
As my past, present and future
Were extinguished as her fragile limbs bent

I finger swiped out one grape
From my youngest seed's mouth that day
It was the second down under
That proved a security blockade

Her jaw locked on my finger
I securely pried my knuckle out
It wasn't until I saw the warm blood, milky fluid, and mucus
Sea spray foam ooze from her nostrils and mouth
That I distinctly understood
What death's uncivilized patience were all about

Every death inviting second that passed
With no vital air to her lungs, heart or brain
Was an authentic confirmation
That no fresh memories would ever be created again

Dead baby in arm
Through Lucifer, the motherfu**er with the black hood, the twilight
zone and
Two red lights I zoomed
Miraculously, they even let me into the emergency room
Black man, bloody mess, no life response
We reserve the right to refuse,
Neither shirt nor shoes

Our heart began to beat
Simultaneously that night
As they yanked the plugs, ceased the drugs and
Took a test drive on life

Some think I am a hero
For my actions that fateful day
My true mates and I think I'm a scared father
Who would exchange my final breath for
My children any moment in the same way
Those mothers have been doing since
Before we could proclaim or refrain all day every day

Besides
If I am truly a knighted hero
Instead of a mad drunken fellow or just plain bloody lucky dope
The coast is now clear to
Salvage shreds of my dreams as well as every once of my hopes

23. Too young to say no, and
Too old to care
Too black to give up, and
Too close to let go

Precious Reader,

Life is precious and short. You may always find yourself short on luck, short on your rent, short on your patience, and short on a whole lengthy tangible list of other tangibles and intangibles. When death comes to cash in a debt, and all your resources have been temporarily allocated and you were exceptionally short on proclaiming your love, sincerity, responsibility or obligation to anyone; you will never be able to recover the deficit. Take control of each moment, stand up straight, look them squarely in the eye, amplify your voice and make time stand still while you stand and deliver.

Azure Moods & Mocha Kisses

I'd like to thank you
For being love, being love
Loving me in spite
Of myself and
Did I ever tell you
How much I loved you
Absent of you
I masked my tears
With dreams of happier years
Moments paralyzed in time
Asking the same questions as to
Why, this, now
And I shoulda, coulda, but I didn't
Didn't make time stand still
Long enough to say it well
Say it well, I
Love You
Unconditionally

I'd like to thank you for being love,
For being love, but I must ask
Why,
Why does this unconditional love thing
Bind so strong
It foreshadows my intentions and
Forgives unasked wrongs
You say you'd like to thank me
For love being,
In reality its continually
Becoming

Cause your azure moods defined
In your slightest thoughts and gestures
Is the grace and humility
That knows no measure
The grace and humility that knows
No measure
And I shoulda, coulda, but I didn't
Didn't make time stand still
Long enough to say it well
Say it well, I
Love You
Unconditionally

Remember Holidays
I do
Remember Birthdays
I do
Remember good days
I do
Remember Mocha Kisses
I do
Remember sweet blues
I do
Remember love
I do

Remember our first introductions
I do
Remember our lasting conversations
I do
Remember our first moonlight
I do
Remember capturing sunsets
I do

Remember the giggle that invites the laughter
I do
Remember the gentle caress
That protects against despair
I do

Before forever with you we were
Broke, hungry and afraid
Too young to say no and
Too old to care
Too Black to give up and
Too close to let go

Baby, before forever with you I was
Too hot to handle and
Too cold to hold
Too independent to gamble on love and
Too fragile disguised as bold
Too rigid to bend gracefully and
Too stubborn to mold
Too poetic to listen and
Too thuggish to be told, but
Before with you forever unfolds
Before with you forever unfolds
And I shoulda, coulda, but I didn't
Didn't make time stand still
Long enough to say it well
Say it well, I
Love You
Unconditionally

Casting aside fear
I submerged myself in
Your words of
"Baby don't worry about it"
Cuz who eva said
Love don't pay the rent
Has never been graced to
Bask in your presence
Behold, the mere essence
Of you lingers
In the air
Creating atmospheres
Of light and sound with no
One but you and me in it
Spin it one more time
For old times sake
And take this Love in my place
For God has chosen you
To spend the rest
Of his life with
And I shoulda, coulda, but I didn't
Didn't make time stand still
Long enough to say it well
Say it well, I
Love You
Unconditionally

Yes, spit it one more time
For old time's sake
For not even all of
God's Love can replace
By his Will, Mercy, Unconditional

Love and Grace
The eventual reunion with you
I eternally await
Baby I Love You, I love you
Beyond the legacy you have bore
That are clothed in my name
Baby I Love You, I love you
Beyond the memories cherished and
Wrong directions changed
Baby I Love You, I love you
Beyond the value and enrichment
To my pitiful life you've reclaimed
Baby I Love You, I love you
Beyond the decomposing spirits and
Resurrected souls we've became
And I shoulda, coulda, but I didn't
Didn't make time stand still
Long enough to say it well
Say it well, I
Love You
Unconditionally

And I wish
I could close my eyes and
Wish upon a star and
Call you back to me
And call you back to me
And call you
Back
To
Me

24. I write for
A score, a dime, raised five
Underground railroad teachers and conductors
Who decode colonized minds, who
De-code
Colonized
Minds

Precious Reader,

So here we are at the invitation of completion. I elected to save this piece for my final reflection against the traditional lure of placing it within the introductory portions of our encounter. For those who have braved the terrain to gather the entire prior "pieces of myself" we already share a resounding intimate familiar. We have "history" and "chemistry" if you will! In an effort to include those unaccustomed to leading with their heart and spirit, I indulge the primary school question of why do you write, what inspires you to write or who or what sustains you to write with a sophisticated domesticated written response. I believe Talib Qweli said it best on the Reflection Eternal album, *I don't write for the streets, I write for the people living in them.* Likewise, there are multiple daily invitations, reminders, reflections and condemnations as to the vibrant, life-sustaining and progress-generating means, ways, rationale and "reasons" to write. I hope you've enjoyed a glimpse of mine until we reunite. I believe Langston Hughes once stated, *My poems don't live on the page, they just rest there until they can reside in a live reading or performance.* I couldn't agree more and anxiously await the opportunity to generate births and rebirths of my Devine Style vs Demonic Word Play along the hot stage hostage continuum.

Indefinite Peace and continued blessings!
NKB

WRITE FOR I

I
Compose
What I comprise
I virtually visualize
An eye for an eye,
And here lies the lies

But when I critically analyze
When I critically analyze
I write for
I

But that's not all
Because when I transpire

I write for
For a dime raised five
Years old *"Bumba Ye"* cousins
Who answer the call to war cries

I write for
For a score raised five
Years old *convicted felon* daddies and brothers
Who are self-confined to the street life

I write for
For a score, a dime raised five
Years old *single parent* mommies and sisters
Who are just struggling and striving to get by

I write for
For a score, a dime raised five
Years old *underground railroad* teachers and conductors
Who decode colonized minds, who
De-code
Colonized
Minds

I write for
For two score raised five
Years old *Big Mamas* and *Grand Papas*
Who are the *adoption, foster care and separation* lifelines

And even though you may
Subconsciously criticize
I am they and they
Substantially am I

Lo and behold
You already mold me and
I already told you
I

Compose
What I comprise
I virtually visualize
An eye for an eye,
And here lies the lies

But what I respectfully realize
What I respectfully realize

I write for
For forty-five years old Big Mama's and Grandfathers, for
For thirty-five years old Underground Railroad Teachers and
Conductors, for
For thirty-five years old single parent Mothers and Sisters, for
For twenty-five years old convicted felon Fathers and Brothers, for
For fifteen years old uprising Sons, Daughters, Nieces, Nephews,
Cousins and Others

For them, for
For we, for
For you, for
For me, for
For I, for
For I always
Have a good reason

For them, for
For we, for
For you, for
For me, for
For I, for
For I do not
Owe you
An explanation